Y0-EIJ-075

WIT & WISDOM OF WOMEN

BY EMILY MILLS

Hallmark

INTRODUCTION

Since the beginning of time, women have been on
the front lines of art, of innovation, of war, of love, of life.
They are artists, athletes, leaders, scholars, sisters, mothers,
and wives. They have fueled a global community of acceptance
and belonging. Their influence inspires us to grow,
to change, to question, to challenge, and—above all—
to celebrate. This little volume celebrates the magnificent
impact of the lives, the work, the sacrifice, and the success
of some of the greatest women of all time. They are
tough. They are witty. They are wise.
They are women.

"I am a woman above everything else."

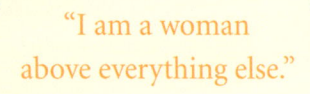

JACQUELINE KENNEDY

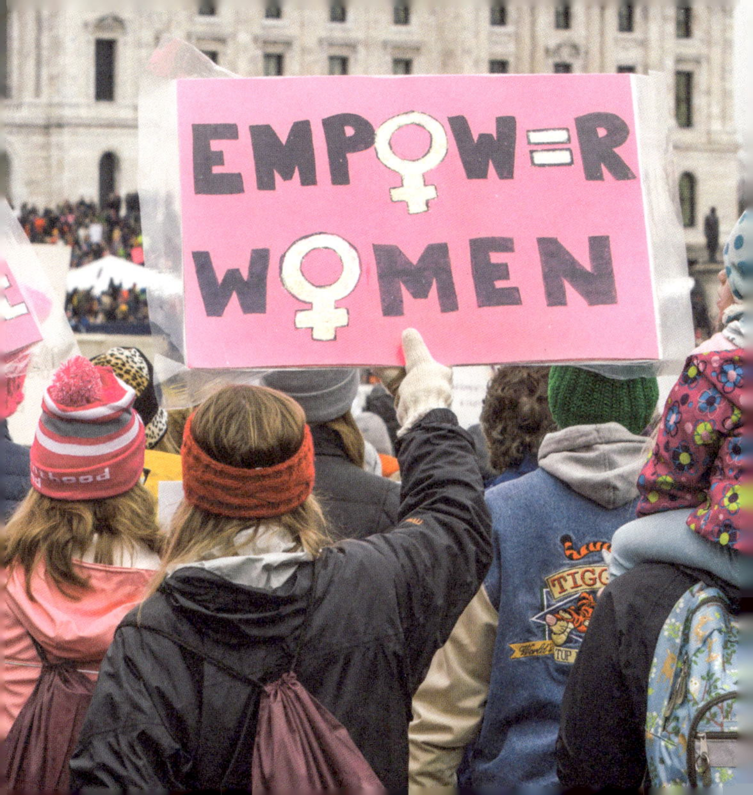
EMPOWER
WOMEN

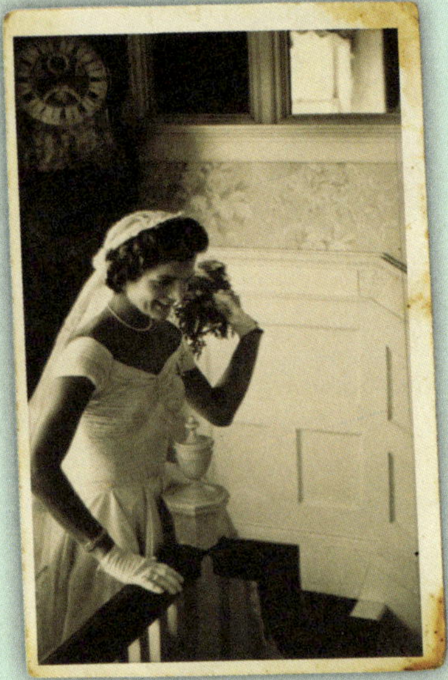

FACT

Apart from being one of America's most beloved first ladies, Jacqueline Kennedy Onassis also played an influential role in preserving American history. Not only did she implement a historic restoration of the White House, but she also played a crucial role in saving Grand Central Station in New York City from being torn down in 1975.

"You may not always have a comfortable life. And you will not always be able to solve all the world's problems at once. But don't ever underestimate the impact you can have, because history has shown us that courage can be contagious, and hope can take on a life of its own."

MICHELLE OBAMA

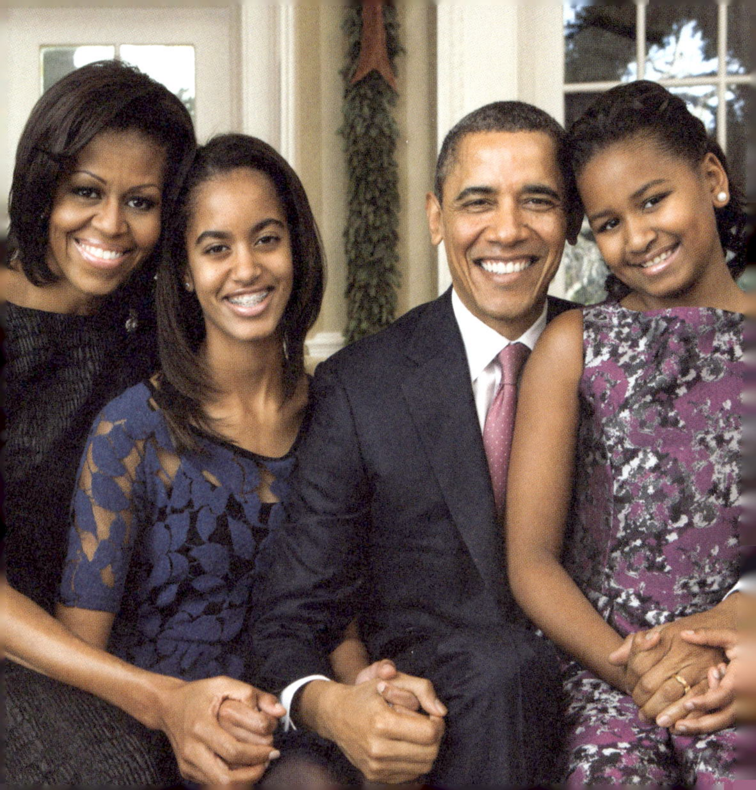

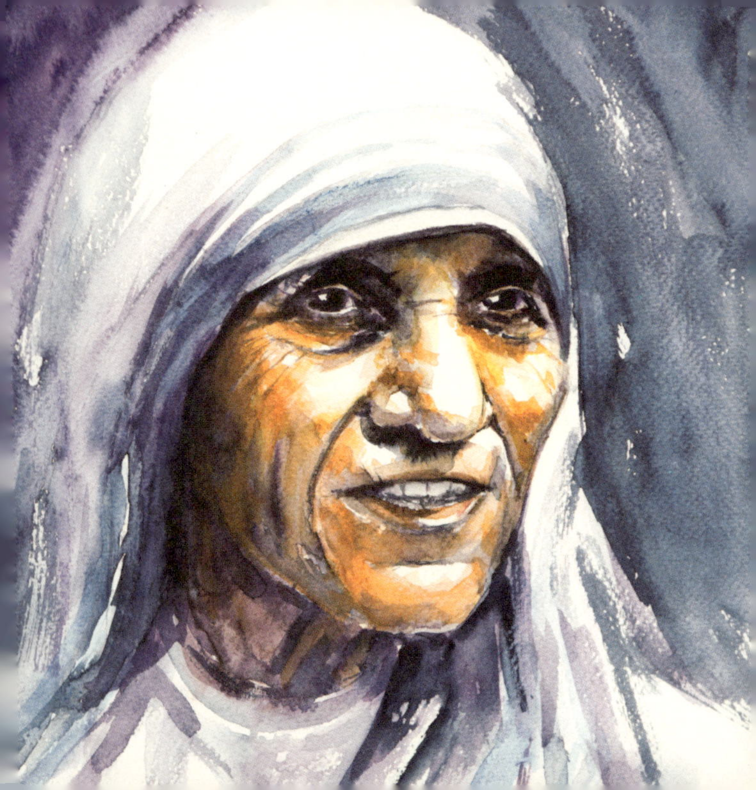

"I alone cannot change the world,
but I can cast a stone across the waters
to create many ripples."

MOTHER TERESA

> "You would Remember the Ladies."
>
> ABIGAIL ADAMS

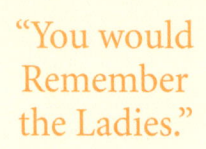

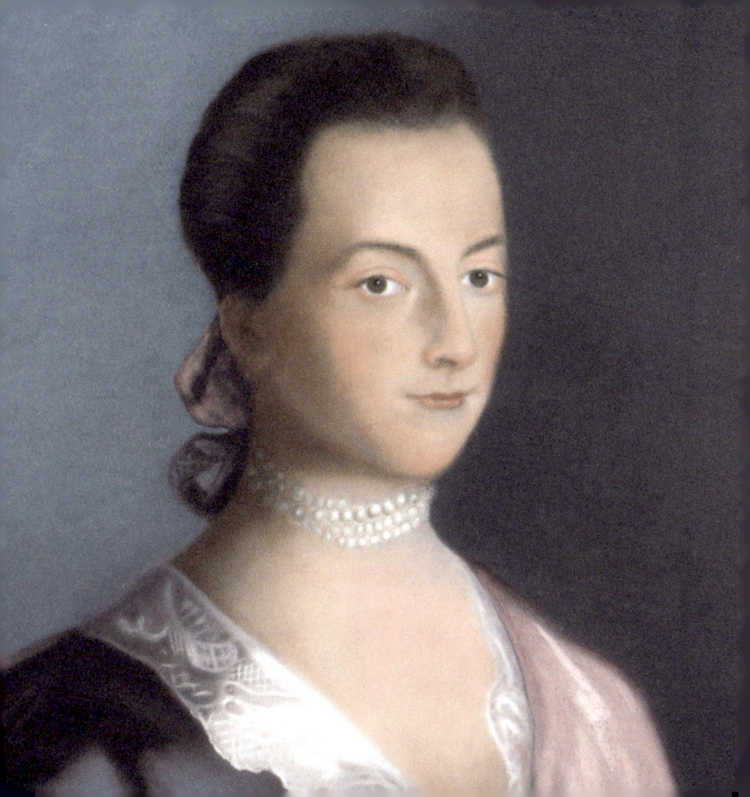

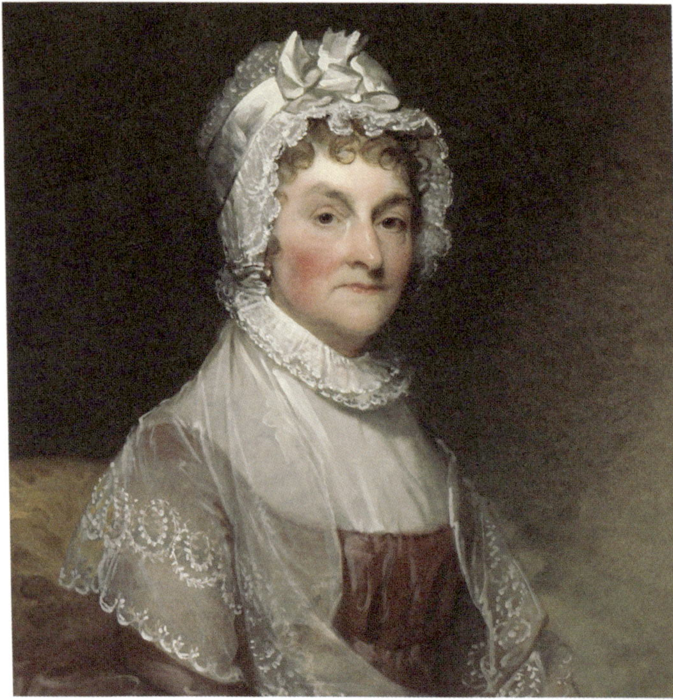

| PROFILE #1 | NOTABLE WOMEN |

ABIGAIL ADAMS (1744-1818)

As Second Lady and First Lady of the United States,
Abigail Adams's influence knew no bounds.
Her husband, John Adams, often wrote her,
asking for advice and guidance on many political matters.
When John was elected President, Abigail became so
politically active that she was often referred to as
"Mrs. President." She fought tirelessly for women's
property rights and educational opportunities, all while
raising her sibling's, in-law's, and own children's children.

"You must never be fearful
about what you are doing
when it is right."

ROSA PARKS

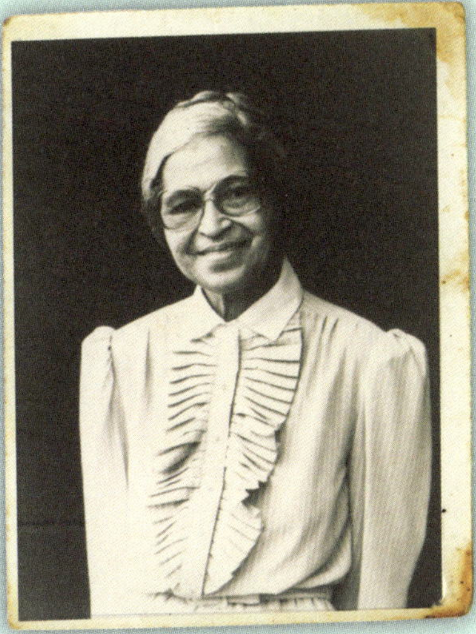

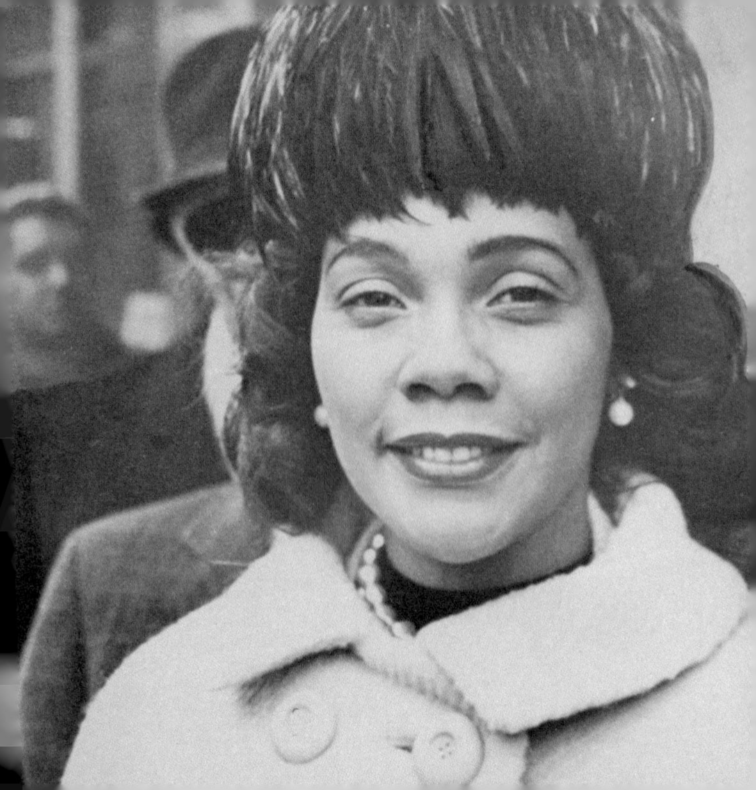

"The woman power of this nation
can be the power which makes us whole."

CORETTA SCOTT KING

"Self-knowledge is no guarantee of happiness, but it is on the side of happiness and can supply the courage to fight for it."

SIMONE DE BEAUVOIR

> **FACT**

Simone de Beauvoir, author and philosopher,
graduated college at the age of seventeen
and went on to be the youngest person to pass
the *agrégation* in philosophy, an incredibly difficult
nationwide French exam, at the age of twenty-one.

"I like to make people a little uncomfortable. It encourages them to examine who they are and why they think the way they do."

SALLY MANN

"We are not interested in the possibilities of defeat;
they do not exist."

QUEEN VICTORIA

"I am my own muse.
The subject I know best."

FRIDA KAHLO

PROFILE #2   NOTABLE WOMEN

FRIDA KAHLO (1907-1954)

Frida Kahlo was born in Coyocoán, Mexico City, where she grew up in a cobalt blue home now called La Casa Azul. The house is presently used as a museum dedicated to her life and work. She began painting in 1925 after being seriously injured in a bus accident and continued to work until her death. Throughout that time, she had an unconventional relationship with a fellow painter, Diego Rivera, whom she met during her time in school. Today, she is recognized as a symbol for feminism and female creativity.

FACT

Frida Kahlo created a total of 143 paintings.
Of those, 55 are self-portraits.

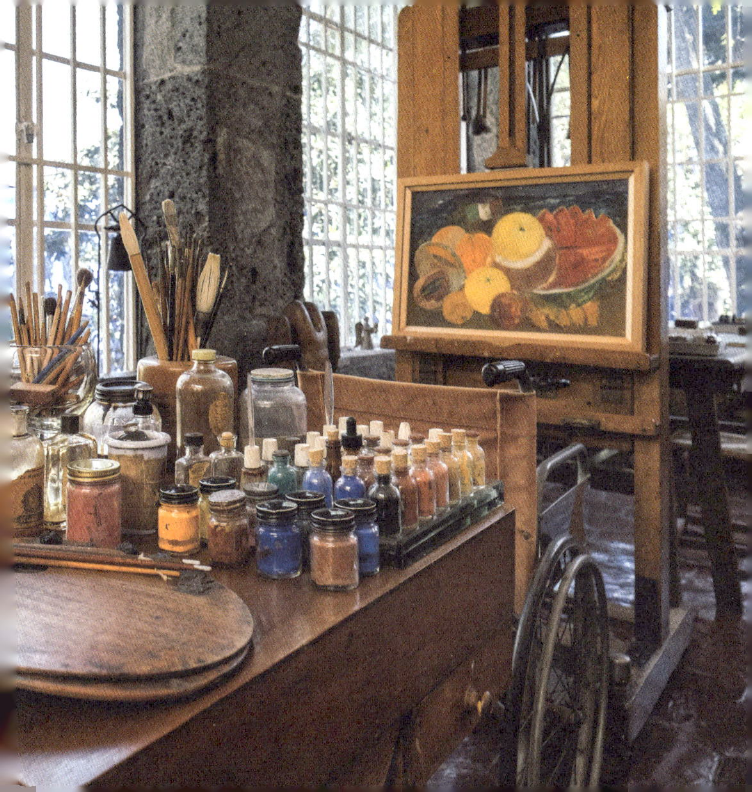

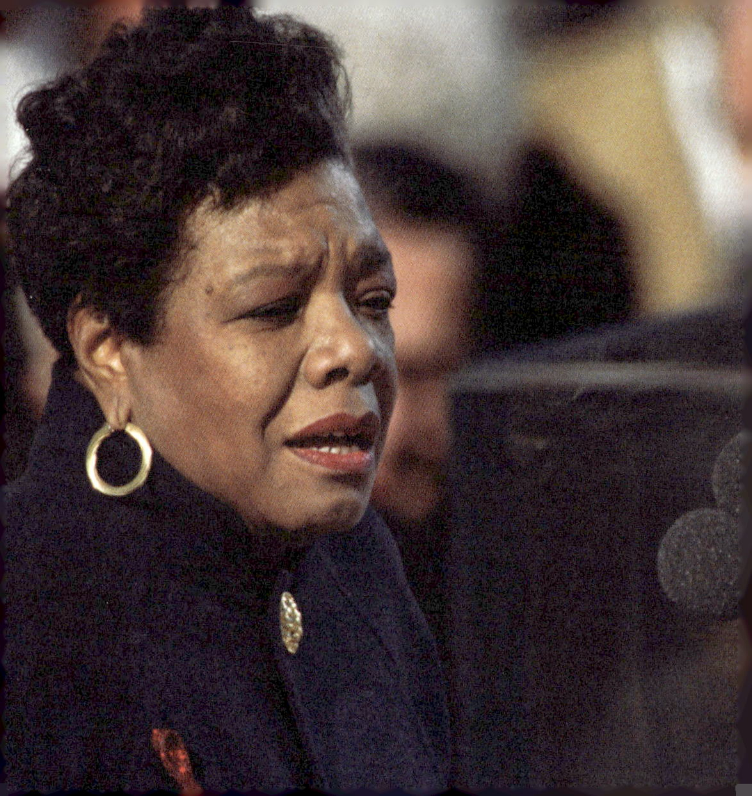

"You see, we may encounter
many defeats, but we must not
be defeated."

MAYA ANGELOU

| PROFILE #3 | NOTABLE WOMEN |

MARILYN MONROE (1926-1962)

Norma Jean Mortenson was born in Los Angeles, California. Her younger years were riddled with various caretakers and foster parents because of her mother's severe mental health issues and her father's complete absence. By her twentieth birthday, she began modeling swimsuits and the world began to take notice. Monroe's acting career commenced when she signed a contract with 20th Century Fox. Not too long after, on February 23rd, 1956, she legally changed her name to Marilyn Monroe. Throughout her lifetime, she acted in twenty-four movies and continued to model, eventually becoming an icon for sex and glamor.

"It's nice to be included in people's fantasies but you also like to be accepted for your own sake."

MARILYN MONROE

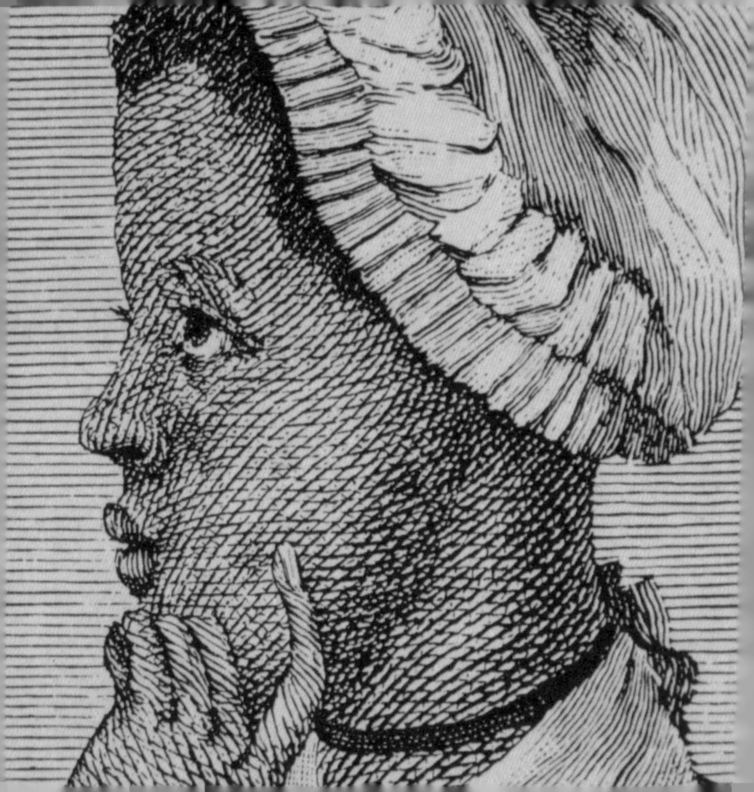

"The world is a severe schoolmaster, for its frowns are less dangerous than its smiles, and it is a difficult task to keep in the path of wisdom."

PHILLIS WHEATLEY

"When the whole world is silent, even one voice becomes powerful."

MALALA YOUSAFZAI

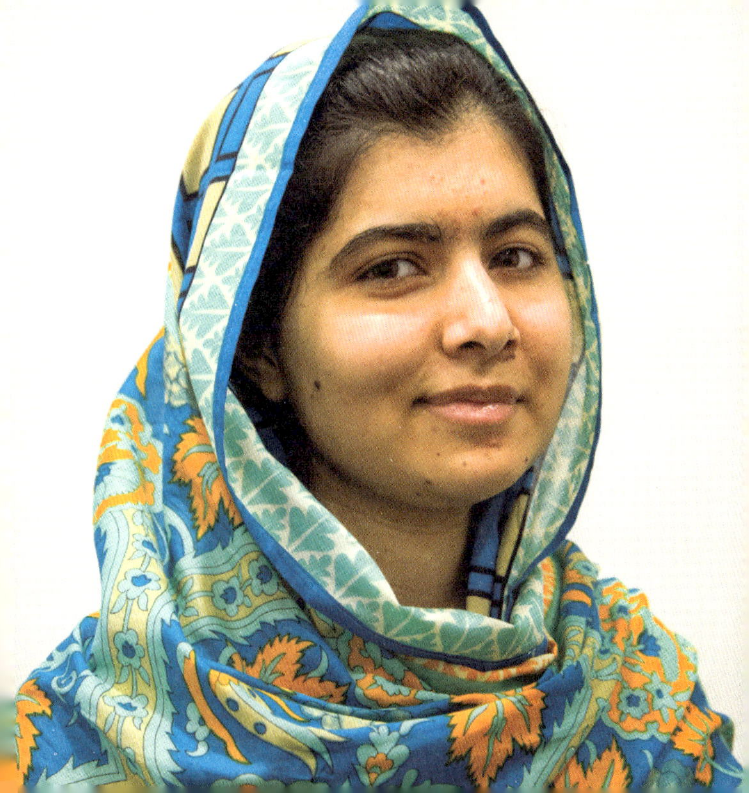

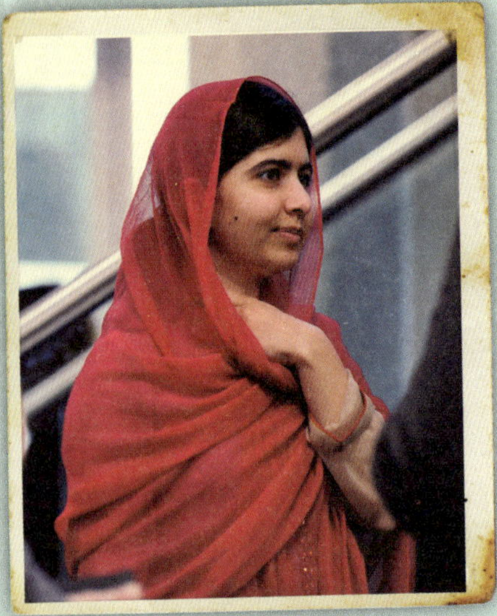

FACT

In 2012, Malala Yousafzai was shot in the head by a Taliban gunman for defending girls' rights to attend school. She survived, and on her sixteenth birthday, she spoke in front of the United Nations about the importance of education for all children. In 2014, she became the youngest recipient of the Nobel Peace Prize at age seventeen.

"Luck has nothing to do with it,
because I have spent many, many hours,
countless hours, on the court working
for my one moment in time,
not knowing when it would come."

SERENA WILLIAMS

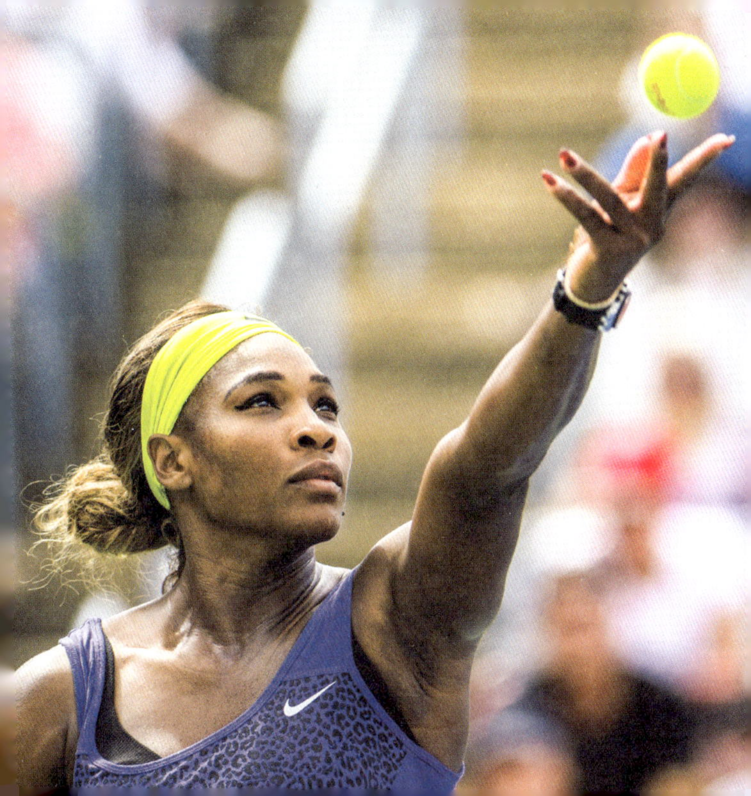

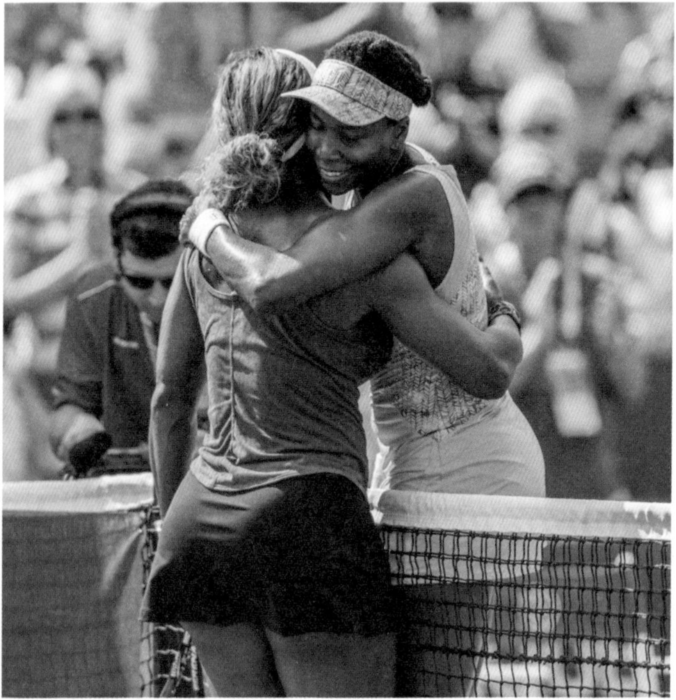

| PROFILE #4 | NOTABLE WOMEN |

SERENA WILLIAMS (1981-)

By age three, Serena Williams had already picked up a tennis racquet. Not long after, her family relocated to Compton, California, from her birthplace in Michigan. Williams's father pushed his five girls to aspire to greatness by encouraging them to participate in athletics to keep them safe from the streets. After years of training and competing, both Serena and her sister Venus became professional tennis players. In 2017, Serena became the number-one ranked female tennis player in the world, with twenty-three Grand Slam titles. Her twenty-third title was earned after defeating Venus.

"I know I have the body of a weak, feeble woman;
but I have the heart and stomach of a king, and of a king of England, too."

QUEEN ELIZABETH I

"The worst evil that you can do, psychologically, is to laugh at yourself. That means spitting in your own face."

AYN RAND

"There are two ways of spreading light: to be the candle or the mirror that receives it."

EDITH WHARTON

FACT

Edith Wharton was the first woman to win
a Pulitzer Prize for literature in 1921
for *The Age of Innocence*.

"Give a girl an education and introduce her properly into the world, and ten to one but she has the means of settling well, without further expense to anybody."

JANE AUSTEN

"The essential dilemma of my life is between my deep desire to belong and my suspicion of belonging."

JHUMPA LAHIRI

> **FACT**

Betty Friedan is credited with triggering the second wave of American feminism with her book *The Feminine Mystique* in 1963.

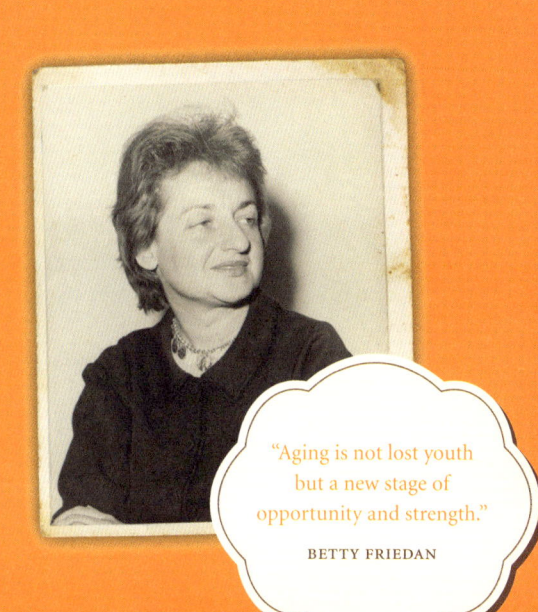

"Aging is not lost youth but a new stage of opportunity and strength."

BETTY FRIEDAN

"These experiences are really gifts that force us to step to the right or left in search of a new center of gravity. Don't fight them. Just find a new way to stand."

OPRAH WINFREY

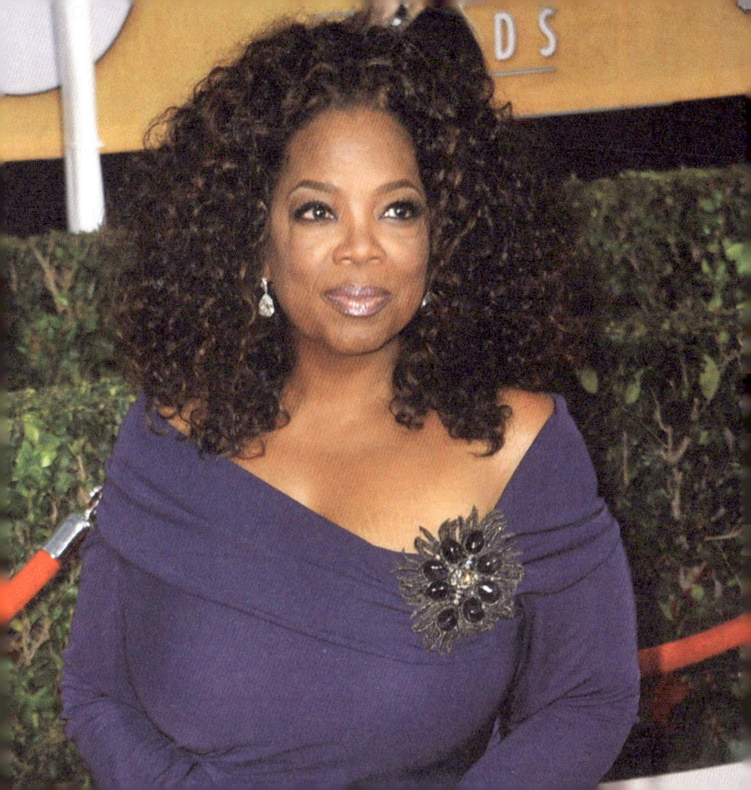

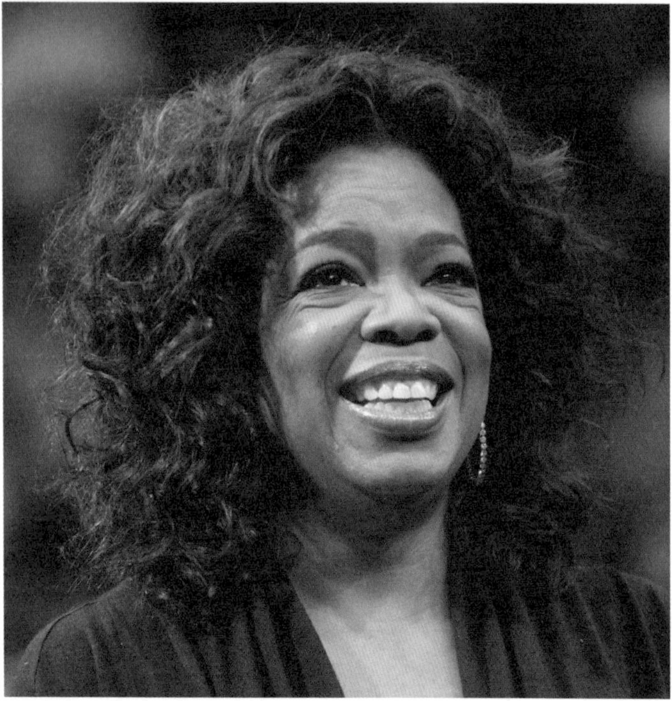

PROFILE #5 | NOTABLE WOMEN

OPRAH WINFREY (1954-)

Orpah Gail Winfrey's birth name, from the Book of Ruth, became translated to Oprah when she was very young. Throughout her difficult childhood, she lived with her mother in poverty, and is a survivor of physical and sexual abuse. In her early teens, she moved in with her strict father to escape the hardship of her younger years. After attending Tennessee State University, Oprah began working as a news anchor. She was criticized for being too sensitive in her style, so she was eventually transferred to a talk show program. This talk show was just the beginning of her success. She later began her own program, *The Oprah Winfrey Show*, which lasted twenty-five seasons, from 1986 until 2011. She was nominated for an Academy Award for her role in *The Color Purple*. She is one of the richest self-made women of all time.

"Don't you ever apologize
for the way your eyes refuse
to stop shining."

SARAH KAY

"I really don't think
I need buns of steel.
I'd be happy with
buns of cinnamon."

ELLEN DEGENERES

FACT

Natalie Portman missed the premiere of *Star Wars: Episode I — The Phantom Menace*, in which she played Padmé Amidala, because she was studying for her high school final exams. A few years later, she graduated from Harvard in 2003 with honors. According to her 140 IQ score, she classifies as genius.

"I'm afraid of everything. But maybe when you're afraid of everything, it sort of seems like you're scared of nothing."

NATALIE PORTMAN

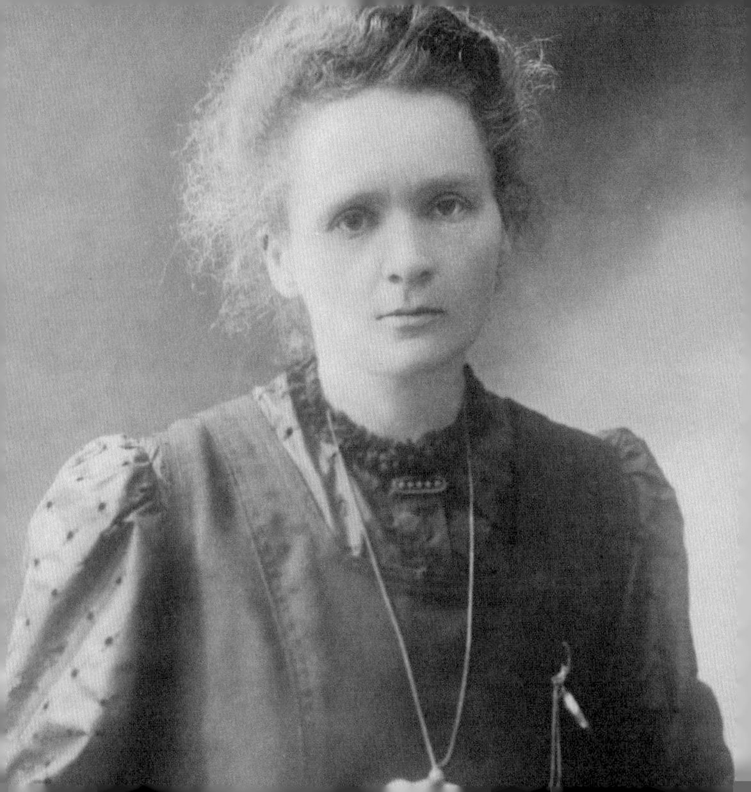

"Life is not easy for any of us, but what of that?
We must have perseverance and above all
confidence in ourselves. We must believe
that we are gifted in something, and that this thing,
at whatever cost, must be attained."

MARIE CURIE

"It isn't where you came from, it's where you're going that counts."

ELLA FITZGERALD

| PROFILE #6 | NOTABLE WOMEN |

ELLA FITZGERALD (1917-1996)

The "First Lady of Song" began her journey toward becoming one of the world's most famous jazz artists bouncing between troubled homes. She moved to New York at a young age and aspired to become a dancer. To support her family, however, Fitzgerald worked as a lookout for a local brothel. In 1934, she entered and won her first entertainment contest at the Apollo Theater in Harlem, where she blew the audience away with her voice. From there, her career took off. Ella Fitzgerald became one of the biggest names in the jazz world and a pioneer of scat improvisation.

"Confidence is 10 percent hard work and 90 percent delusion."

TINA FEY

"Never be afraid to stop traffic."

IRIS APFEL

"Imagination is not only the uniquely human capacity to envision that which is not, and therefore the fount of all invention and innovation. In its arguably most transformative and revelatory capacity, it is the power that enables us to empathise with humans whose experiences we have never shared."

J.K. ROWLING

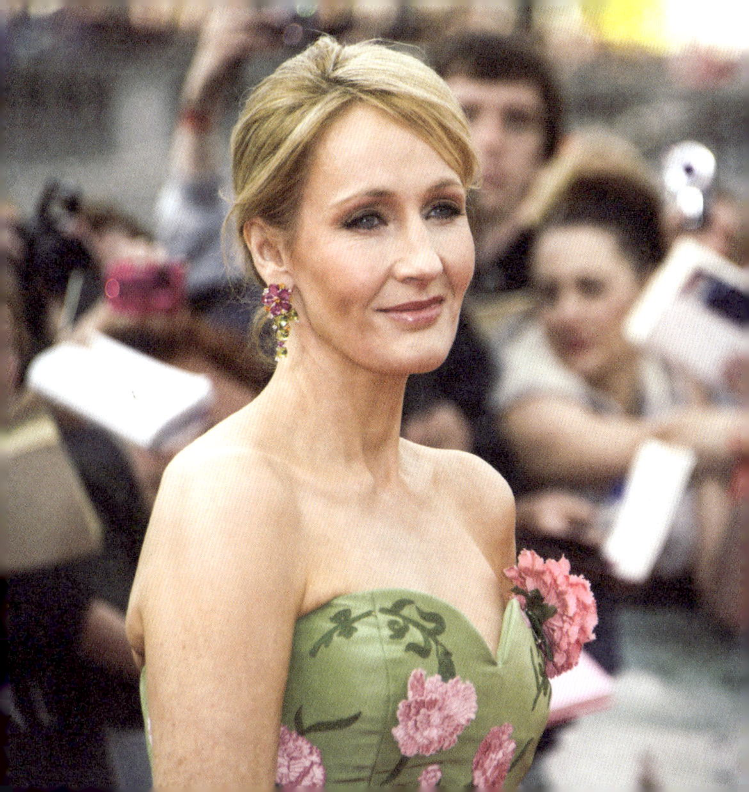

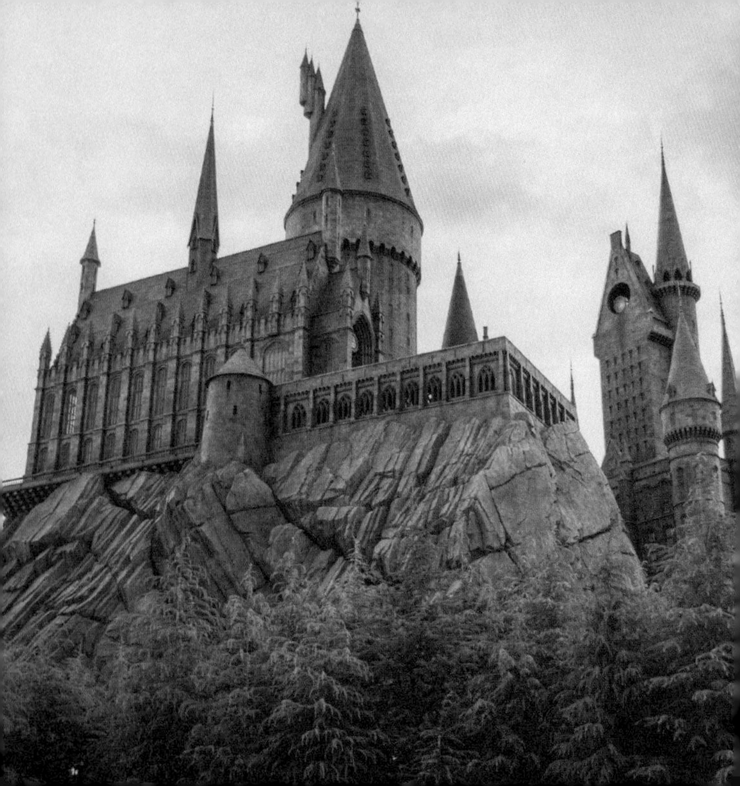

FACT

J.K. Rowling began her enchanting *Harry Potter* series on a napkin, while she was traveling to London on a train. She had many interesting processes for coming up with names within the book. "Quidditch" was developed by filling five notebook pages with fictitious "Q" words.

"Dreams are lovely. But they are just dreams.
Fleeting, ephemeral, pretty. But dreams do not
come true just because you dream them.
It's hard work that makes things happen.
It's hard work that creates change."

SHONDA RHIMES

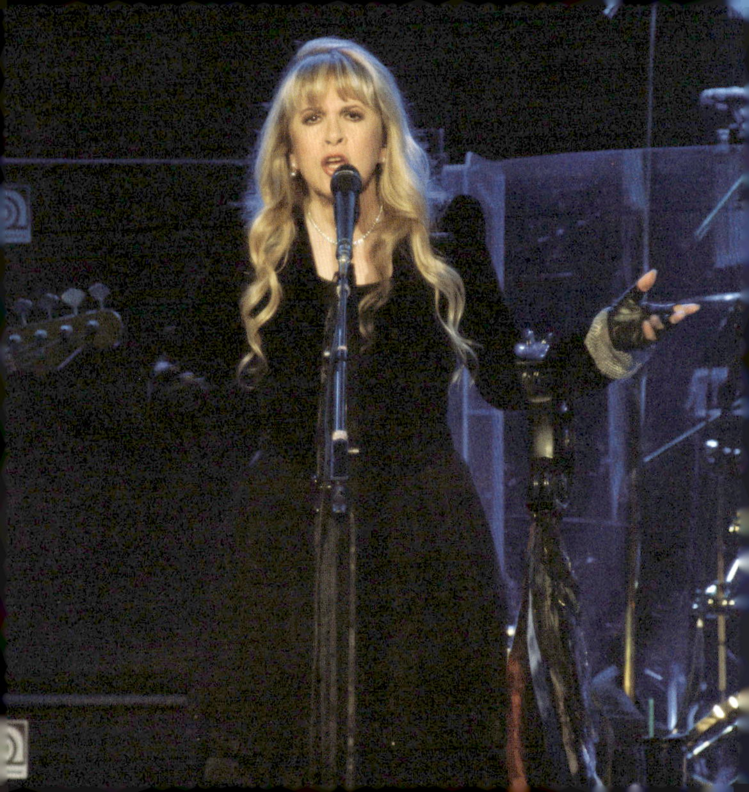

"Your graciousness is what carries you.
It isn't how old you are, how young you are,
how beautiful you are, or how short your skirt is.
What it is, is what comes out of your heart.
If you are gracious, you have won the game."

STEVIE NICKS

| PROFILE #7 | NOTABLE WOMEN |

STEVIE NICKS (1948-)

Throughout her childhood, Stephanie Lynn Nicks moved from state to state because of her father's job as a corporate executive. Eventually, the family landed in California, where Nicks attended high school. There, she met her future lover and bandmate, Lindsay Buckingham. After high school, Nicks attended college for a brief time before dropping out and joining a band called Fritz with Buckingham. In 1975, the duo was sought out and signed by another group named Fleetwood Mac, and the newly formed band became an instant success. Nicks later broke away from Fleetwood Mac to do some solo work, but during that time experienced problems with alcohol and drug addiction. After many tough years, she became sober and reunited with Fleetwood Mac once again in 1997.

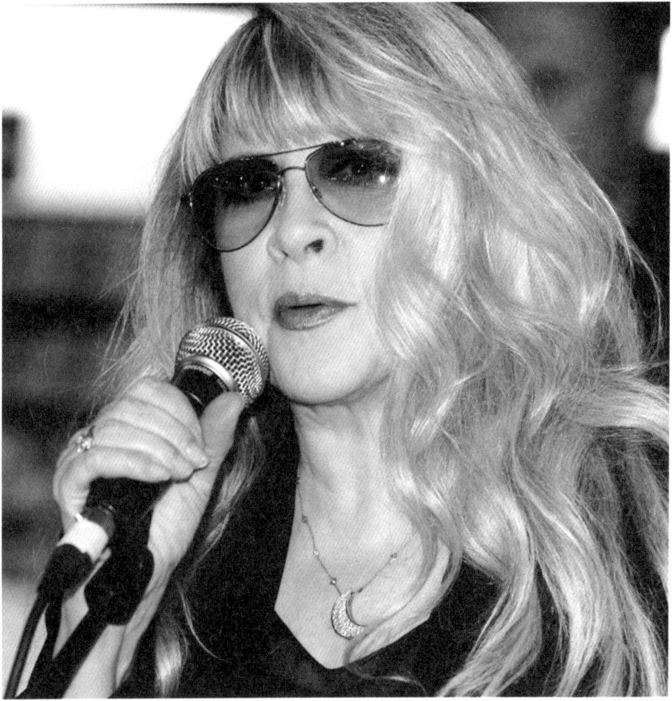

> "A strong woman looks a challenge dead in the eye and gives it a wink."
>
> GINA CAREY

"Don't feel stupid if you don't like what everyone else pretends to love."

EMMA WATSON

"No one can make you feel inferior without your consent."

ELEANOR ROOSEVELT

| PROFILE #8 | NOTABLE WOMEN |

ELEANOR ROOSEVELT (1884-1962)

Credited with transforming the role of first lady into a position of political leadership, Eleanor Roosevelt became one of the twentieth century's most influential female diplomats of the United States. After the deaths of both her parents before she had even reached her teenage years, Roosevelt was sent to England to attend boarding school. In 1905, she married Franklin D. Roosevelt, her distant cousin, who became president in 1933. As first lady, she spoke out for human rights, working both domestically and internationally to support women, children, and the poor. She later became chair of the United Nations' Human Rights Commission.

FACT

Amelia Bloomer was a women's rights activist who is often associated with women's "bloomers," a loose-fitting undergarment that featured a split leg, as she was a strong proponent for change in women's fashion.

"Let men be compelled to wear our dress for a while, and we should soon hear them advocating a change, as loudly as they now condemn it."

AMELIA BLOOMER

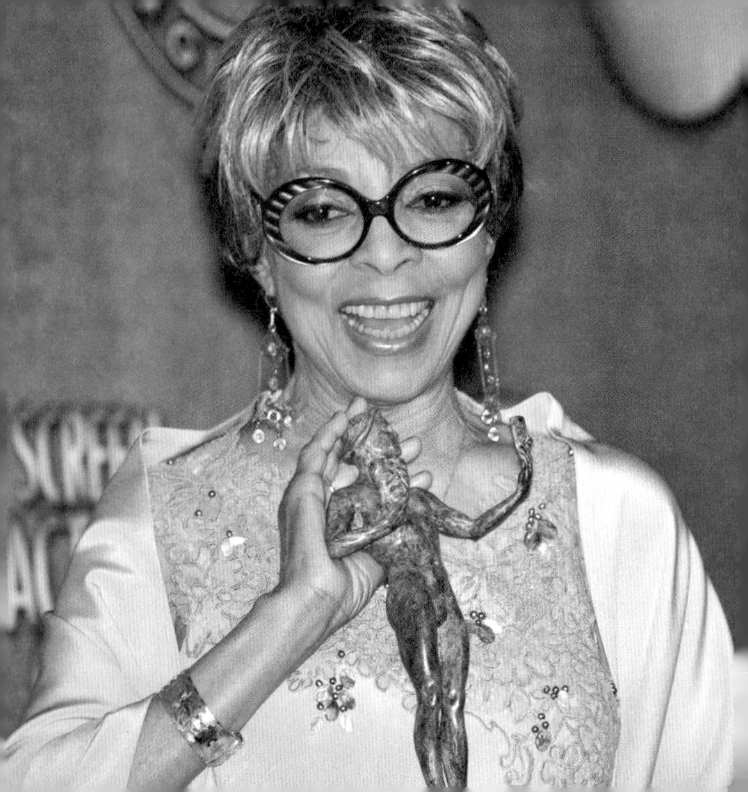

"The kind of beauty I want most is the hard-to-get kind that comes from within—strength, courage, dignity."

RUBY DEE

"The world will see you
the way you see you,
and treat you the way
you treat yourself."

BEYONCÉ

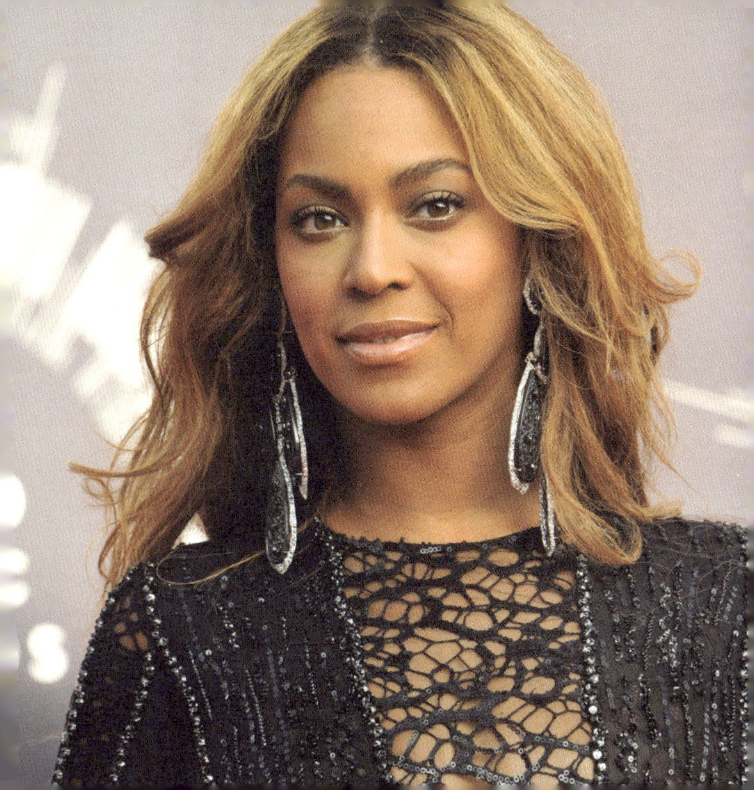

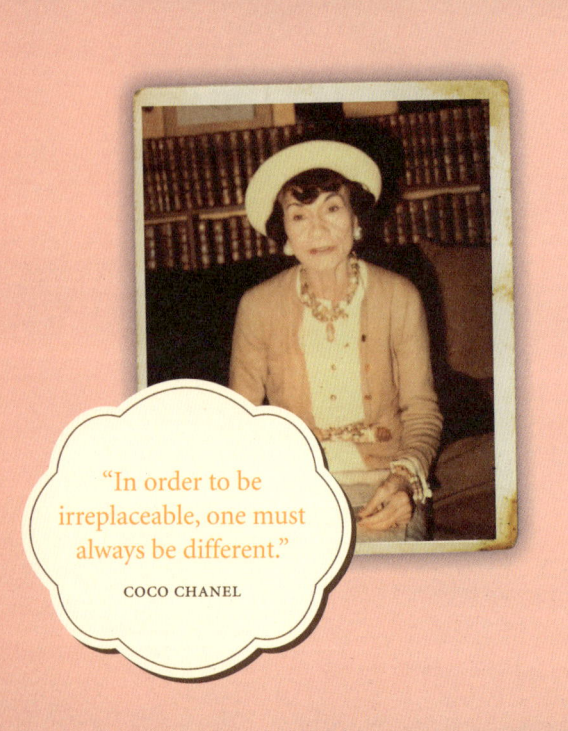

"In order to be irreplaceable, one must always be different."

COCO CHANEL

FACT

Coco Chanel, who began her career as a licensed hatmaker, went on to become one of the most recognizable and classic fashion designers in history. Chanel No.5 perfume remains the bestselling perfume of all time. She is also credited with being the first designer to produce suits for women.

"Only you know who you were born to be,
and you need to be free to be that person."

RUBY ROSE

"It is the ultimate luxury to combine passion and contribution. It's also a very clear path to happiness."

SHERYL SANDBERG

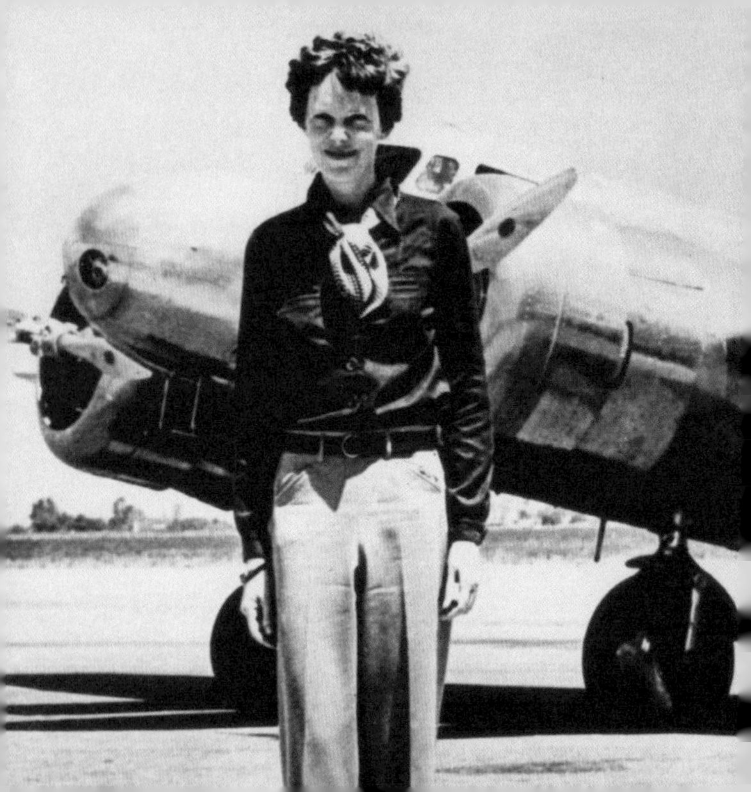

"Never interrupt someone doing what you said couldn't be done."

AMELIA EARHART

FACT

Amelia Earhart was not only influential as a pilot; she also designed flying clothing that was advertised in *Vogue*.

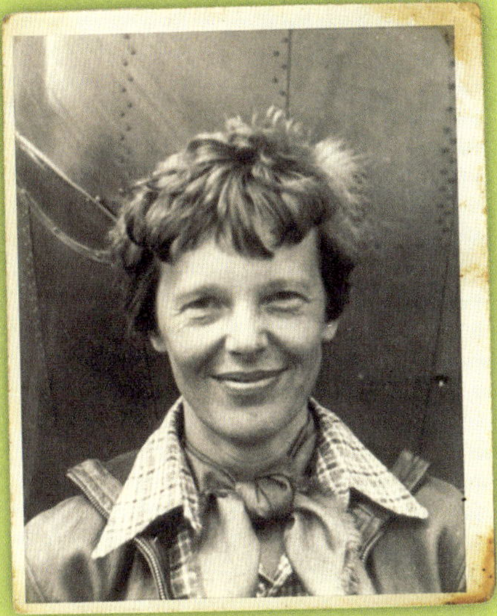

"Keep your face to the sunshine and you cannot see the shadows."

HELEN KELLER

"Energy rightly applied and directed will accomplish anything."

NELLIE BLY

| PROFILE #9 | NOTABLE WOMEN |

FLORENCE NIGHTINGALE (1820-1910)

Born in Italy to British parents, Florence Nightingale is known for abandoning the elite social status and affluence of her family to fulfill her calling as a nurse. During the Crimean War, she joined a team of nurses at a base camp to help treat British and French soldiers. While there, she began to recognize the deplorable conditions of many healthcare centers of the time. Nightingale wrote about the issues and championed staffing adequate numbers of nurses, improving sanitation, and focusing on patient care. Her writings triggered healthcare reform worldwide.

"I attribute my success to this: I never gave or took an excuse."

FLORENCE NIGHTINGALE

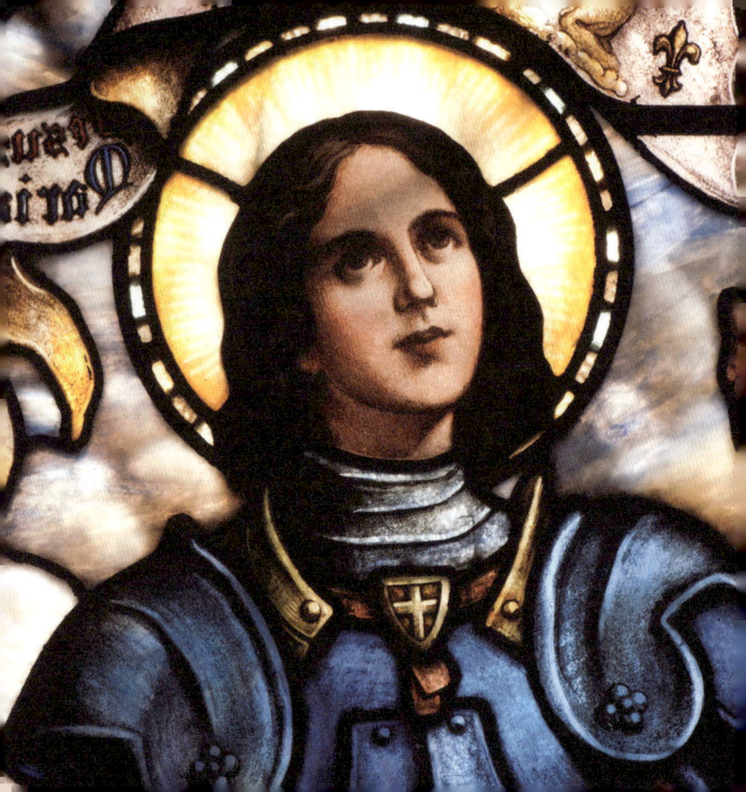

"One life is all we have,
and we live it as we believe in living it.
But to sacrifice what you are
and to live without belief;
that is a fate more terrible than dying."

JOAN OF ARC

FACT

Clara Barton is known for founding the American Red Cross, but she was also the first female clerk in the United States Patent Office.

"I have an almost complete disregard of precedent and a faith in the possibility of something better. It irritates me to be told how things have always been done…. I defy the tyranny of precedent. I cannot afford the luxury of a closed mind."

CLARA BARTON

"If you want something said, ask a man; if you want something done, ask a woman."

MARGARET THATCHER

"Expect the unexpected,
and whenever possible,
be the unexpected."

LYNDA BARRY

"Make your mess
your message."

ROBIN ROBERTS

"Growth and comfort don't coexist."

GINNI ROMETTY

FACT

Frances E. Willard became the first female college president in the United States, at Evanston College for Ladies, in 1871. The college later merged with Northwestern University, and Willard became the first Dean of Women.

"I would not waste my life in friction when it could be turned into momentum."

FRANCES E. WILLARD

"I used my imagination to make the grass whatever color I wanted it to be."

WHOOPI GOLDBERG

"Authenticity is the daily practice of letting go of who we think we're supposed to be and embracing who we are."

BRENÉ BROWN

"When you put love out in the world it travels, and it can touch people and reach people in ways that we never even expected."

LAVERNE COX

FACT

In third grade, Laverne Cox's teacher told her mother, "Your son is going to end up in New Orleans wearing a dress if you don't get him into therapy right away." Today, she may be best-known for her Emmy-nominated role in *Orange Is the New Black* and is one of the most influential voices supporting the transgender community. And, indeed, she did end up in a dress…on the cover of *Time Magazine* and many other leading publications.

> "Easy lives make boring people."
>
> RONDA ROUSEY

> "You can do anything you want, even if you are being told negative things. Stay strong and find motivation."
>
> — MISTY COPELAND

"Life shrinks or expands in proportion to one's courage."

ANAIS NIN

"The winds, the sea, and the moving tides
are what they are. If there is wonder and beauty
and majesty in them, science will discover these qualities.
If they are not there, science cannot create them.
If there is poetry in my book about the sea, it is not because
I deliberately put it there, but because no one could write
truthfully about the sea and leave out the poetry."

RACHEL CARSON

| PROFILE #10 | NOTABLE WOMEN |

RACHEL CARSON (1907-1964)

Environmental activism in the twentieth century was largely influenced by the writings and work of Rachel Carson. She began her career as a marine biologist and worked for the United States Fish and Wildlife Service. This developed into multiple books that addressed topics such as underwater research, the effects of pesticides, and climate change. Her book *Silent Spring* prompted changes in mindset about the environment and begged humans to question what right we have to control and destroy nature.

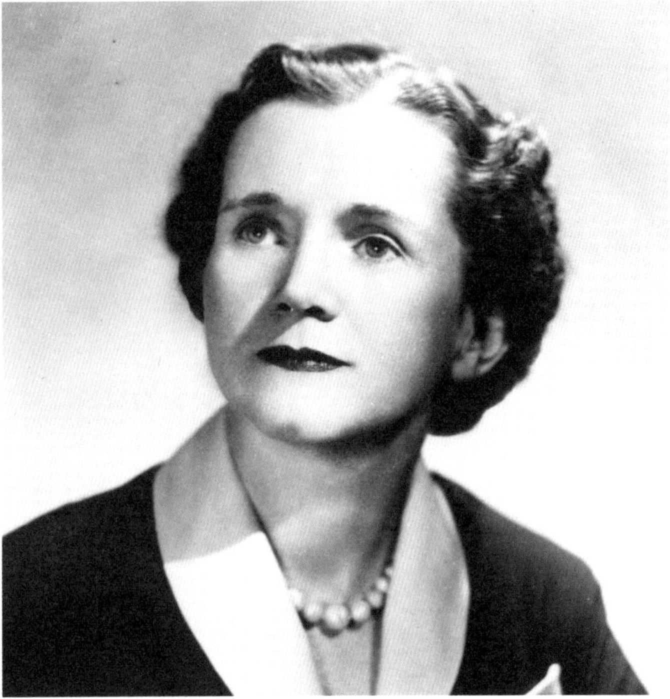

"I believe that the privilege of a lifetime is being who you are, truly being who you are, and I've spent far too long apologizing for that."

VIOLA DAVIS

"I am only interested in the ideas that become obsessive and make me feel uneasy. The ideas that I'm afraid of."

MARINA ABRAMOVIC

> **FACT**

Shirley Chisholm was the first black woman elected into Congress and was also the first African American to run for president in 1972.

"If they don't give you a seat at the table, bring a folding chair."

SHIRLEY CHISHOLM

"Ambition is not a four-letter word,
and women have to embrace that."

TORY BURCH

"I have bursts of being a lady, but it doesn't last long."

SHELLEY WINTERS

"The secret of staying young is to live honestly,
eat slowly, and lie about your age."

LUCILLE BALL

FACT

Lucille Ball was not only known for her iconic role in the television comedy *I Love Lucy*; she was also the first woman to manage a major Hollywood studio.

"I don't believe in aging. I believe in forever altering one's aspect to the sun."

VIRGINIA WOOLF

"I've always dreamed of growing up to be Amy Poehler."

AMY POEHLER

"If you got it, flaunt it. If you don't got it, flaunt it."

MINDY KALING

> "Women are repeatedly accused of taking things personally. I cannot see any other honest way of taking them."
>
> MARYA MANNES

PROFILE #11 | NOTABLE WOMEN

MERYL STREEP (1949-)

From an early age, Meryl Streep set out to be a performer. After graduating from Vassar College, she attended Yale Drama School and then began acting in Broadway shows throughout the 1960s and 70s. Her work in film took off with a role in *Julia* in 1977. Since then, she has starred in many award-winning productions such as *Sophie's Choice*, *The Iron Lady*, and *Mamma Mia!*

"Integrate what you believe into every single area of your life.
Take your heart to work, and ask the most and best of everybody else, too."

MERYL STREEP

"Weightlessness is a great equalizer."

SALLY RIDE

FACT

Sally Ride was the first American woman to travel with NASA into space. She was later inducted into the National Women's Hall of Fame and the Astronaut Hall of Fame.

"Courage in women is often mistaken for insanity."

A PSYCHIATRIST ON ALICE PAUL, SUFFRAGIST

"If the first woman God ever made was strong enough to turn the world upside down all alone, these women together ought to be able to turn it back, and get it right side up again!"

SOJOURNER TRUTH

"Old-fashioned ways which no longer apply to changed conditions are a snare in which the feet of women have always become readily entangled."

JANE ADDAMS

PROFILE #12 | NOTABLE WOMEN

JANE ADDAMS (1860-1935)

Activist, feminist, and Nobel Peace Prize winner, Jane Addams developed a passion for helping those around her at a young age. In 1889, Addams and her friend Ellen Gates Starr opened the Hull House in Chicago, primarily to assist immigrants in the area. Soon, it expanded to offer childcare services, a soup kitchen, educational classes, and more. Addams later became the first female president of the National Conference of Social Work and served as the president of the Women's International League for Peace and Freedom. In 1931, she was awarded the Nobel Peace Prize, making her the first American woman to receive the honor.

"When you're that successful, things have a momentum, and at a certain point you can't really tell whether you have created the momentum or it's creating you."

ANNIE LENNOX

"Don't call me a saint. I don't want to be dismissed so easily."

DOROTHY DAY

PROFILE #13 | NOTABLE WOMEN

PAULA SCHER (1948-)

The field of graphic design was revolutionized by the work of Paula Scher. In 1970, she graduated from the Tyler School of Art and started working with CBS Records in its advertising department. While there, Scher is estimated to have designed approximately one hundred fifty album covers per year. After developing her style, Scher began to do work for many major companies, especially within New York City. She has worked with the Museum of Modern Art (MoMA), New York City Ballet, and The Public Theater, and also created the logo for Microsoft: Windows 8.

"If I get up every day with the optimism that I have the capacity for growth, then that is success to me."

PAULA SCHER

"Every minute [is] a chance to change the world…"

DOLORES HUERTA

"Each person is born with very individual qualities and potential. We as a society owe it to women to create a truly supportive environment in which they, too, can grow and move forward."

DIANA, PRINCESS OF WALES

FACT

Before becoming known for her skills as a chef, Julia Child was a basketball player at Smith College and also worked for the predecessor of the Central Intelligence Agency.

"Life itself is the proper binge."

JULIA CHILD

"Tell them that as soon as I can walk I'm going to fly."

BESSIE COLEMAN

| PROFILE #14 | NOTABLE WOMEN |

BESSIE COLEMAN (1892-1926)

Inspired in her early twenties by stories of World War I pilots, Bessie Coleman started to set goals of flying for herself. Coleman's race and gender created hurdles that she was determined to overcome. Because the United States flight schools would not admit her, she was forced to look elsewhere to fulfill her dreams. Coleman taught herself French and traveled to Caudron Brothers School of Aviation in France, where she became the first black woman to earn a pilot's license. She died at the young age of thirty-four during one of her aerial performances—but not before inspiring many and setting new precedents within the world of aviation.

"I try to give people a different way of looking at their surroundings. That's art to me."

MAYA LIN

> "We have to go after the truth...
> Let us be fierce and dangerous
> about the truth."
>
> LOUISE ERDRICH

PROFILE #15 | NOTABLE WOMEN

HELEN HAYES (1900-1993)

Helen Hayes MacArthur, an American actress, had a career in film and on stage that lasted nearly eighty years. She is one of just twelve people to receive an Emmy, a Grammy, an Oscar, and a Tony. But her life's work did not stop at acting. Hayes dedicated herself to philanthropic work as well, founding the Helen Hayes Hospital for rehabilitation, holding a chair on the board of directors for the Girl Scouts of the USA, and donating time and funds to the Riverside Shakespeare Company.

"Age is not important unless you're cheese."

HELEN HAYES

"If the stable gate is closed, climb the fence."

JULIE KRONE

FACT

Julie Krone was the first female jockey to win a Triple Crown race in 1993.

"The work of today is the history of tomorrow, and we are its makers."

JULIETTE GORDON LOW

PROFILE #16   NOTABLE WOMEN

JULIETTE GORDON LOW (1860-1927)

Nicknamed "Daisy," Juliette Gordon Low was the founder of the Girl Scouts. In 1911, she began meeting with Robert Baden-Powell, who founded the Boy Scouts. Drawing on inspiration from the work he had done, Low formed some of the first troops. The program gained in popularity thanks to the remarkable effect it had on empowering girls, becoming the largest such organization of its kind in the United States. Upon her death, she was buried in her Girl Scout uniform, as she had wished. In the pocket was a telegram from the national office proclaiming her "the best Girl Scout of them all."

FACT

Georgia O'Keeffe's favorite place to create artwork was in the backseat of a Model-A Ford.

"I found I could say things with color and shapes that I couldn't say any other way— things I had no words for."

GEORGIA O'KEEFFE

"For me, sitting still is harder than any kind of work."

ANNIE OAKLEY

"I try to maintain a healthy dose of daydreaming, to remain sane."

FLORENCE WELCH

> "I believe that as much as you take, you have to give back. It's important not to focus on yourself too much."
>
> NICOLE KIDMAN

"We cannot run and ask permission
every time we want to do something new."

LORETTA C. FORD

| PROFILE #17 | NOTABLE WOMEN |

HARRIET TUBMAN (1822-1913)

Known as one of the most famous "conductors" of the Underground Railroad, Harriet Tubman played a major role in the success of the abolitionist movement. After escaping her own enslavement, she helped to lead hundreds of the enslaved to freedom. Tubman also worked as a spy for the Union Army during the Civil War.

> "He set the North star in the heavens; he meant I should be free."
>
> HARRIET TUBMAN

"My mother told me to be a lady. And for her that meant be your own person, be independent."

RUTH BADER GINSBURG

"Participate, find your nook....You don't have to be a lawyer, but you have to be an involved person. You have to care enough about things to do something about them. It doesn't have to be politics. It can be your church, your school, your community center; however, you want to be involved. What you cannot do is ignore things."

JUSTICE SONIA SOTOMAYOR

"Don't sit down and wait for the opportunities to come....Get up and make them!"

MADAM C.J. WALKER

32 USA

PROFILE #18 | NOTABLE WOMEN

MADAM C.J. WALKER (1867-1919)

Born the child of two recently freed slaves, Sarah Breedlove became known as Madam C. J. Walker after starting her own hair care line for black women. She was incredibly successful with this venture, making today's equivalent of more than a million dollars. Walker used this money to support philanthropic causes such as the YMCA, educational scholarships, homes for the elderly, and the NAACP.

"The lessons from the peace process are clear; whatever life throws at us, our individual responses will be all the stronger for working together and sharing the load."

QUEEN ELIZABETH II

"Nothing can really prepare you for the sheer, overwhelming experience of what it means to become a mother. It's full of complex emotions of joy, exhaustion, love, and worry, all mixed together."

CATHERINE, DUCHESS OF CAMBRIDGE

"Talent is everywhere,
it only needs the opportunity."

KATHRINE SWITZER

FACT

In 1967, Kathrine Switzer was the first woman
to run the Boston Marathon as a numbered participant.
Five years later, women were officially
welcomed into the race.

| PROFILE #19 | NOTABLE WOMEN |

JANE GOODALL (1934-)

Jane Goodall is noted for her respected contributions to the scientific community. Her tireless work observing chimpanzees led to many discoveries about the species, including the finding that chimpanzees create tools, something thought to be unique to humans. She is the author of numerous published articles and five books.

"The greatest danger to our future is apathy."

JANE GOODALL

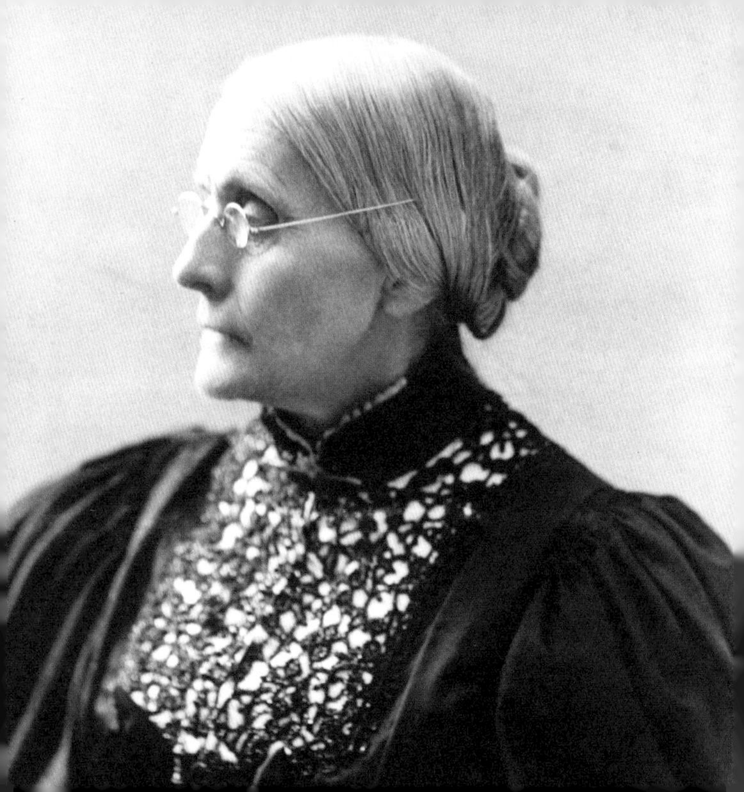

> "Failure is impossible."
>
> SUSAN B. ANTHONY

Wishing you a fabulous journey! I know you will succeed at anything you put your mind to!

S.B.

If you enjoyed this book
or it has touched your life in some way,
we'd love to hear from you.

Please write a review at Hallmark.com,
e-mail us at booknotes@hallmark.com,
or send your comments to:

Hallmark Book Feedback
P.O. Box 419034
Mail Drop 100
Kansas City, MO 64141